The American Way

The American Way

Selections from the public
addresses and papers of

Franklin D. Roosevelt

Edited by DAGOBERT D. RUNES

PHILOSOPHICAL LIBRARY

New York

The numerals appearing at the foot of each excerpt
indicate the date of the respective paper or speech.

Printed in the United States of America by
The Colonial Press, Inc., Clinton, Mass.

Prefatory Note

This little book has been designed for the many persons here as well as abroad who would like to get a clearer picture of the inner motives, the personal outlook and the social philosophy of the late President.

The editor has gone through the massive body of the available papers and utterances of Mr. Roosevelt and has drawn from them statements of the underlying principles and the fundamental faith that seem to have impelled the actions of this unusual man. These statements are to be found within the texture of the many discussions on various phases of public policy. Sometimes as a brief assertion of a compelling cause of action, sometimes almost as a casual aside, the words lead beyond the momentary issue to assertion of an abiding faith.

This faith, combined with a deep-felt social philosophy and concern for human needs and aspirations, has from Jefferson and Lincoln to Roosevelt shaped the American way of life.

D.D.R.

Contents

The American Way

I affirm that life in the centuries that lie ahead must be based on positive and permanent values.

The value of love will always be stronger than the value of hate; since any nation or group of nations which employs hatred eventually is torn to pieces by hatred within itself.

The value of a belief in humanity and justice is always stronger in any land than the value of belief in force, because force at last turns inward and if that occurs each man or group of men is finally compelled to measure his strength against his own brother.

The value of truth and sincerity is always stronger than the value of lies and cynicism. No process has yet been invented which can permanently separate men from their own hearts and consciences or prevent them from seeing the results of their own false ideas as time rolls by. You cannot make men believe that a way of life is good when it spreads poverty, misery, disease and death. Men cannot be everlastingly loyal unless they are free.

9

We acclaim today the American Way.

We are determined to live in peace and to make that peace secure. We are determined to follow the paths of free peoples to a civilization worthy of free men.

IV-15-1940

The Rights of the Common Man

In the early days of the Republic our life was simple. There was little need of formal arrangements, or of government interest, or action, to insure the social and economic well-being of the American people. In the life of the pioneer, sympathy and kindly help, ready cooperation in the accidents and emergencies of the frontier life were the spontaneous manifestation of the American spirit. Without them the conquest of a continent could never have been made.

Today that life is gone. Its simplicity has vanished and we are each and all of us, whether we like it or not, parts of a social civilization which ever tends to greater complexity. And in these later days, the imperiled well-being, the very existence of large numbers of our people, have called for measures of organized Government assistance which the more spontaneous and personal promptings of a pioneer generosity could never alone have obtained. Our country is indeed passing through a period which is urgently in need of ardent protectors of the rights of the common man. Mechanization of industry and mass production have put unparalleled power in the hands of the few. No small part of our problem today is to bring the fruits of this mechanization and mass production to the people as a whole.

VI-10-1936

*   *   *

History proves that dictatorships do not grow out of strong and successful governments, but out of weak and helpless ones. If by democratic methods people get a government strong enough to protect them from fear and starvation, their democracy succeeds; but if they do not, they grow impatient. Therefore, the only sure bulwark of continuing liberty is a government strong enough to protect the interests of the people, and a people strong enough and well enough informed to maintain its sovereign control over its government.

We are a rich Nation; we can afford to pay for security and prosperity without having to sacrifice our liberties in the bargain.

IV-14-1938

*   *   *

There must be no place in the post-war world for social privileges for either individuals or nations.

XI-7-1941

*   *   *

No business is above Government; and Government must be empowered to deal adequately with any business that tries to rise above Government.

IX-2-1940

*   *   *

Government has a final responsibility for the well-being of its citizenship. If private cooperative endeavor fails to provide work for willing hands and relief for the unfortunate, those suffering hardship from no fault of their own have a right to call upon the Government for aid; and a government worthy of its name must make fitting response.

I-3-1938

*   *   *

Our economic and social system cannot deny the paramount right of the millions who toil and the millions who wish to toil, to have it function smoothly and efficiently. After all, any such system must provide efficiently for distributing national resources and serving the welfare and happiness of all who live under it.

XI-4-1938

*   *   *

We have come a long way. But we still have a long way to go. There is still today a frontier that remains unconquered—an America unreclaimed. This is the great, the nation-wide frontier of insecurity, of human want and fear. This is the frontier—the America—we have set ourselves to reclaim.

VIII-15-1938

*   *   *

Once old age was safe because there was always something useful which men and women, no matter how old, could do to earn an honorable maintenance. That time is gone; and some new kind of organized old-age insurance has to be provided.

VII-8-1938

*   *   *

The sense of human decency is happily confined to no group or class. You find it in the humblest home. You find it among those who toil, and among the shop-keepers and the farmers of the nation. You find it, to a growing degree, even among those who are listed in that top group which has so much control over the industrial and financial structure of the nation. Therefore, this urge of humanity can by no means be labeled a war of class against class. It is rather a war against poverty and suffering and ill-health and inse-curity, a war in which all classes are joining in the interest of a sound and enduring democracy.

VII-19-1940

*   *   *

It is right—wholly right—to prosecute criminals. But that is not enough, for there is the immense added task of working for the elimination of present and fu-ture crime by getting rid of evil social conditions which breed crime. Good government can prevent a thousand crimes for every one it punishes.

XI-4-1938

*   *   *

Our national purchasing power is the soil from which comes all our prosperity. The steady flow of wages to our millions of workers is essential if the products of our industry and of our farmers are to be consumed.

Our far-sighted industrial leaders now recognize that a very substantial share of corporate earnings must be paid out in wages, or the soil from which these industries grow will soon become impoverished. Our farmers recognize that their largest customers are the workers for wages, and that farm markets cannot be maintained except through widespread purchasing power.

The unemployment problem is one in which every individual and every economic group has a direct interest. It is a problem whose discussion must be removed from the field of prejudice to the field of logic. We shall find the solution only when we have the facts, and having the facts, accept our mutual responsibilities.

The inherent right to work is one of the elemental privileges of a free people. Continued failure to achieve that right and privilege by anyone who wants to work and needs work is a challenge to our civilization and to our security. Endowed, as our nation is, with abundant physical resources, and inspired as it should be with the high purpose to make those resources and opportunities available for the enjoyment of all, we approach this problem of re-employment with the real hope of finding a better answer than we have now.

XI-14-1937

*   *   *

Of course we shall continue to strengthen all the dynamic reforms in our social and economic life; to keep the processes of democracy side by side with the necessities and possibilities of modern industrial production.

Of course we shall continue to make available the good things of life created by the genius of science and technology—to use them, however, not for the enjoyment of the few but for the welfare of all.

For there lies the road to democracy that is strong.

Of course we intend to preserve and build up the land of this country—its soil, its forests and its rivers —all the resources with which God has endowed the people of the United States.

Of course we intend to continue to build up the bodies and the minds of the men, women and children of the Nation—through democratic education and a democratic program for health.

For there lies the road to democracy that is strong.

Of course we shall continue our efforts to prevent economic dictatorship as well as political dictatorship.

Of course we intend to continue to build up the morale of this country, not as blind obedience to some leader, but as the expression of confidence in the deeply ethical principles upon which this Nation and its democracy were founded.

For there lies the road to democracy that is strong.

This Nation which has become the industrial leader of the world has the humanity to know that the people of a free land need not suffer the disease of poverty and the dread of not being wanted.

It is the destiny of this American generation to point the road to the future for all the world to see. It is our prayer that all lovers of freedom may join us— the anguished common people of this earth for whom we seek to light the path.

I see an America where factory workers are not discarded after they reach their prime, where there is no endless chain of poverty from generation to generation, where impoverished farmers and farm hands do not become homeless wanderers, where monoply does not make youth a beggar for a job.

I see an America whose rivers and valleys and lakes —hills and streams and plains—the mountains over our land and nature's wealth deep under the earth— are protected as the rightful heritage of all the people.

I see an America where small business really has a chance to flourish and grow.

I see an America of great cultural and educational opportunity for all its people.

I see an America where the income from the land shall be implemented and protected by a Government determined to guarantee to those who hoe it a fair share in the national income.

An America where the wheels of trade and private

industry continue to turn to make the goods for America. Where no businessman can be stifled by the harsh hand of monopoly, and where the legitimate profits of legitimate business are the fair reward of every businessman—big and little—in all the Nation.

I see an America with peace in the ranks of labor.

An America where the workers are really free and—through their great unions undominated by any outside force, or by any dictator within—can take their proper place at the council table with the owners and managers of business. Where the dignity and security of the working man and woman are guaranteed by their own strength and fortified by the safeguards of law.

XI-2-1940

*　　*　　*

It is our duty now to begin to lay plans and determine the strategy for the winning of a lasting peace and the establishment of an American standard of living higher than ever before known. We cannot be content, no matter how high the general standard of living may be, if some fraction of our people—whether it be one-third or one-fifth or one-tenth—is ill-fed, ill-clothed, ill-housed, and insecure.

This Republic had its beginning, and grew to its present strength, under the protection of certain inalienable political rights—among them the right of free speech, free press, free worship, trial by jury, freedom from unreasonable searches and seizures. They were our rights to life and liberty.

As our nation has grown in size and stature, however—as our industrial economy expanded—these political rights proved inadequate to assure us equality in the pursuit of happiness.

We have come to a clear realization of the fact that true individual freedom cannot exist without economic security and independence. "Necessitous men are not free men." People who are hungry and out of a job are the stuff of which dictatorships are made.

In our day these economic truths have become accepted as self-evident. We have accepted, so to speak, a second Bill of Rights under which a new basis of security and prosperity can be established for all, regardless of station, race or creed.

Among these are:

The right to a useful and remunerative job in the industries or shops or farms or mines of the nation;

The right to earn enough to provide adequate food and clothing and recreation;

The right of every farmer to raise and sell his products at a return which will give him and his family a decent living;

The right of every businessman, large and small, to trade in an atmosphere of freedom from unfair competition and domination by monopolies at home or abroad;

The right of every family to a decent home;

The right to adequate medical care and the opportunity to achieve and enjoy good health;

The right to adequate protection from the economic fears of old age, sickness, accident and unemployment;

The right to a good education.

All of these rights spell security. And after this war is won we must be prepared to move forward, in the implementation of these rights, to new goals of human happiness and well-being.

America's own rightful place in the world depends in large part upon how fully these and similar rights have been carried into practice for our citizens. For unless there is security here at home there cannot be lasting peace in the world.

I-12-44

Young America

The vigor of our history comes, largely, from the fact that, as a comparatively young Nation we have gone fearlessly ahead doing things that were never done before. We subdued a wilderness that men said could never be conquered. We established a civilization where others insisted a civilization could not survive. Between 1776 and 1789 we built a Republic, a Government for which, in the extent of its democracy, there had been no precedent—a Government which Royalists declared could not endure.

We did all these things with zest. The very air was exhilarating. We were young; we were getting things done—worthwhile things. And it is part of the spirit of America to believe that now, in our day, we can do equally well in getting things done. Once again, the very air of America is exhilarating.

I, for one, do not believe that the era of the pioneer is at an end; I only believe that the area for pioneering has changed. The period of geographical pioneering is largely finished. But, my friends, the period of social pioneering is only at its beginning. And make no mistake about it—the same qualities of heroism and faith and vision that were required to bring the forces of Nature into subjection will be required—in even greater measure—to bring under proper control the forces of modern society. There is a task which, for importance and for magnitude, calls for the best that you and I have to offer.

There cannot be too many Americans thinking about the future of America. Our country, richly endowed today in body, mind and spirit, still has need of many things. But I am certain that one of its chief needs today is the releasing and the enlistment of the spirit of youth.

IV-13-1936

*   *   *

The pioneers survived by fighting their own fight and by standing together as one man in the face of danger. If we, their descendants, are to meet the dangers that threaten us, we too must be ready to fight our own fight and stand together as one man. In hours of peril the frontiersmen, whatever their personal likes or dislikes, whatever their personal differences of opinion, gathered together in absolute unity for defense. We, in this hour, must have and will have absolute national unity for total defense.

What shall we be defending? The good earth of this land, our homes, our families—yes, and far more. We shall be defending a way of life which has given more freedom to the soul and body of man than ever has been realized in the world before, a way of life that has let men scale whatever heights they could scale without hurting their fellows, a way of life that has let men hold up their heads and admit no master but God.

That way of life has been menaced. We can meet the threat. We can meet it with the old frontier spirit. We can forge our weapons, train ourselves to shoot, meet fire with fire, and with the courage and the unity of the frontiersmen.

It is our pride that in our country men are free to differ with each other and with their Government and to follow their own thoughts and express them. We believe that the only whole man is a free man. We believe that, in the face of danger, the old spirit of the frontiersmen that is in our blood will give us the courage and unity that we must have.

We need that spirit in this hour. We need a conviction, felt deep in us all, that there are no divisions among us. We are all members of the same body. We are all Americans.

The winds that blow through the wide sky in these mountains, the winds that sweep from Canada to Mexico, from the Pacific to the Atlantic—have always blown on free men. We are free today. If we join together now—men and women and children—to face the common menace as a united people, we shall be free tomorrow.

X-2-1940

*   *   *

Our future belongs to us Americans.

It is for us to design it; for us to build it.

In that building of it we shall prove that our faith is strong enough to survive the most fearsome storms that have ever swept over the earth.

In the days and months and years to come, we shall be making history—hewing out a new shape for the future. And we shall make very sure that that future of ours bears the likeness of liberty.

Always the heart and the soul of our country will be the heart and the soul of the common man—the men and the women who never have ceased to believe in democracy, who never have ceased to love their families, their homes and their country.

The spirit of the common man is the spirit of peace and good will. It is the spirit of God. And in His faith is the strength of all America.

XI-2-1940

The Inter-American Order

Universal and stable peace remains a dream. War, more horrible and destructive than ever, has laid its blighting hand on many parts of the earth. But peace among our American nations remains secure because of the instruments we have succeeded in creating. They embody, in great measure at least, the principles upon which, I believe, enduring peace must be based throughout all the rest of the world.

Peace reigns today in the Western Hemisphere because our nations have liberated themselves from fear. No nation is truly at peace if it lives under the shadow of coercion or invasion. By the simple process of agreeing that each nation shall respect the integrity and independence of the others, the New World has freed itself of the greatest and simplest cause of war. Self-restraint and the acceptance of the equal rights of our neighbors as an act of effective good will have given us the peace we have had, and will preserve that peace so long as we abide by this ultimate moral law.

Peace reigns among us today because we have agreed, as neighbors should, to mind our own businesses. We have renounced, each and all of us, any right to interfere in each other's domestic affairs, recognizing that free and independent nations must shape their own destinies and find their own ways of life.

Peace reigns among us today because we have resolved to settle any dispute that should arise among us by friendly negotiations in accordance with justice and equity, rather than by force. We have created effective machinery for this purpose; and we have demonstrated our willingness to have full recourse to that method.

Peace reigns among us because we have recognized the principle that only through vigorous and mutually beneficial international economic relations can each of us have adequate access to materials and opportunities necessary to a rising level of economic well-being for all of our peoples. In every practicable way we are seeking to bring this vital principle to its realization.

We of this hemisphere have no need to seek a new international order; we have already found it. This was not won by hysterical outcries, or violent movements of troops. We do not stamp out nations, capture governments, or uproot innocent people from the homes that they have built. We do not invent absurd doctrines of race supremacy, or claim dictatorship through universal revolution.

The inter-American order was not built by hatred and terror. It has been paved by the endless and effective work of men of good will. We have built a foundation for the lives of hundreds of millions. We have unified these lives by a common devotion to a moral order.

This cooperative peace in the Western Hemisphere was not created by mere wishing; and it will require more than mere words to maintain. In this association of nations, whoever touches any one of us touches us all. We have only asked that the world go with us in the path of peace. But we shall be able to keep that way open only if we are prepared to meet force with force if challenge is ever made against us.

IV-15-1940

* * *

No one group or race in the New World has any desire to subjugate the others. No one nation in this hemisphere has any desire to dominate the others. In the Western Hemisphere no nation is considered a second-class nation.

We know that attempts have been made—we know that they will continue to be made, alas—to divide these groups within a nation, and to divide these nations among themselves.

There are those in the Old World who persist in believing that here in this new hemisphere the Americas can be torn by the hatreds and fears which have drenched the battle grounds of Europe for so many centuries. Americans as individuals, American Republics as nations, remain on guard against those who seek to break up our unity by preaching ancient race hatreds, by working on old fears, or by holding out glittering promises which they know to be false.

"Divide and conquer!" That has been the battle cry of the totalitarian powers in their war against the democracies. It has succeeded on the continent of Europe for the moment. On our continents it will fail.

X-12-1940

*   *   *

Now, more than ever before, we of this American Hemisphere must make plain that these principles, upon which so great a civilization is founded, are vibrant, productive and dynamic. National and international law and morality are not the restraints of weaklings; they are signs of serene strength—confidence in our purpose, and in our ability to maintain independence and democracy.

*   *   *

Our ideal is democratic liberty. Our instrument is honor and friendship. Our method is increased understanding. Our basis is confidence. So and not otherwise, in common effort we safeguard in this new world the great rights of our liberties and build our civilization for the advancement of humanity throughout the world.

IV-14-1938

*   *   *

The faith of the Americas, therefore, lies in the spirit. The system, the sisterhood, of the Americas is impregnable so long as her Nations maintain that spirit.

In that faith and spirit we will have peace over the Western World. In that faith and spirit we will all watch and guard our Hemisphere. In that faith and spirit may we also, with God's help, offer hope to our brethren overseas.

XII-1-1936

Not Bread Alone

We people of America know that man cannot live by bread alone.

We know that we have a reservoir of religious strength which can withstand attacks from abroad and corruption from within.

We people of America will always cherish and preserve that strength. We will always cling to our religion, our devotion to God—to the faith which gives us comfort and the strength to face evil.

*　　*　　*

What this weary world most needs is a revival of the spirit of religion. Would that such a revival could sweep the nations today and stir the hearts of men and women of all faiths to a reassertion of their belief in the Providence of God and the brotherhood of man. I doubt if there is in the world a single problem, whether social, political, or economic, which would not find ready solution if men and nations would rule their lives according to the plain teaching of the Sermon on the Mount.

VI-15-1938

*   *   *

Religion by teaching man his relationship to God, gives the individual a sense of his own dignity and teaches him to respect himself by respecting his neighbors.

I-4-1939

*   *   *

The majority of Americans, whether they adhere to the ancient teaching of Israel or accept the tenets of the Christian religion, have a common source of inspiration in the Old Testament. In the spirit of brotherhood we should, therefore, seek to emphasize all those many essential things in which we find unity in our common Biblical heritage.

If we labor in that spirit may we not hope to attain the ideal put forth by the Prophet Micah: "And what doth the Lord require of thee, but to do justly, and to love mercy, and to walk humbly with thy God?"

III-3-1939

*   *   *

A fervent allegiance to religion is the strongest bulwark of enduring democracy.

XII-12-1942

*   *   *

No matter what the accidents and chances of life may bring in their train, no matter what the changing habits and fashions of the world may effect, the Bible continues to hold its unchallenged place as the most loved, the most quoted and the most universally read and pondered of all the volumes which our libraries contain. It has withstood assaults, it has resisted and survived the most searching microscopic examinations, it has stood every test that could be applied to it and yet it continues to hold its supreme place as the Book of books.

There have been periods when it has suffered stern and searching criticism, but the hottest flame has not destroyed its prevailing and persistent power. We cannot read the history of our rise and development as a Nation, without reckoning with the place the Bible has occupied in shaping the advances of the Republic. Its teaching, as has been wisely suggested, is ploughed into the very heart of the race.

Where we have been truest and most consistent in obeying its precepts we have attained the greatest measure of contentment and prosperity; where it has been to us as the words of a book that is sealed, we have faltered in our way, lost our range-finders and found our progress checked.

X-5-1935

*   *   *

Against enemies who preach the principles of hate and practice them, we set our faith in human love and in God's care for us and all men everywhere.

XII-25-1942

Foreign Tyranny

. . . *In* Europe, many nations, through dictatorships or invasions, have been compelled to abandon normal democratic processes. They have been compelled to adopt forms of government which some call "new and efficient."

They are not new, my friends, they are only a relapse—a relapse into ancient history. The omnipotent rulers of the greater part of modern Europe have guaranteed efficiency, and work, and a type of security.

But the slaves who built the pyramids for the glory of the dictator Pharaohs of Egypt had that kind of security, that kind of efficiency, that kind of corporative state.

So did the inhabitants of that world which extended from Britain to Persia under the undisputed rule of the proconsuls sent out from Rome.

So did the henchmen, the tradesmen, the mercenaries and the slaves of the feudal system which dominated Europe a thousand years ago.

So did the people of those nations of Europe who received their kings and their government at the whim of the conquering Napoleon.

Whatever its new trappings and new slogans, tyranny is the oldest and most discredited rule known to history. And whenever tyranny has replaced a more human form of government it has been due more to internal causes than external. Democracy can thrive only when it enlists the devotion of those whom Lincoln called the common people. Democracy can hold that devotion only when it adequately respects their dignity by so ordering society as to assure to the masses of men and women reasonable security and hope for themselves and for their children.

We in our democracy, and those who live in still unconquered democracies, will never willingly descend to any form of this so-called security of efficiency which calls for the abandonment of other securities more vital to the dignity of man. It is our credo —unshakable to the end—that we must live under the liberties that were first heralded by Magna Charta and placed into glorious operation through the Declaration of Independence, the Constitution of the United States and the Bill of Rights.

VII-9-1940

*　　*　　*

. . . *This* land is great because it is a land of endless challenge. Our country was first populated, and it has been steadily developed, by men and women in whom there burned the spirit of adventure and restlessness and individual independence which will not tolerate opposition.

Ours has been a story, a story of vigorous challenge which has been accepted and overcome—challenges of uncharted seas, of wild forests and desert plains, of raging floods and withering droughts, of foreign tyrants and domestic strife, of staggering problems, social and economic and physical. And we have come out of them the most powerful nation—the freest—in all history.

Today, in the face of this newest and greatest challenge of them all, we Americans have cleared our decks and taken out battle station. We stand ready in the defense of our nation and in the faith of our fathers to do what God has given us the power to see as our full duty.

X-27-1941

* * *

We are fighting today for security and progress and for peace, not only for ourselves but for all men, not only for one generation but for all generations. We are fighting to cleanse the world of ancient evils, ancient ills.

We are inspired by a faith which goes back through all the years to the first chapter of the Book of Genesis,—"God created man in His own image."

We on our side are striving to be true to that divine heritage. We are fighting, as our forefathers have fought, to uphold the doctrine that all men are equal in the sight of God.

There never has been and never can be a successful compromise between good and evil. Only total victory can reward the champions of tolerance and decency and freedom and faith.

I-7-1942

*　　*　　*

We will not, under any threat, or in the face of any danger, surrender the guarantee of liberty our forefathers framed for us in our Bill of Rights.

We hold with all the passion of our hearts and minds to those commitments of the human spirit.

We are solemnly determined that no power or combination of powers of this earth shall shake our hold upon them.

We covenant with each other before all the world that, having taken up arms in the defense of liberty, we will not lay them down before liberty is once again secure in the world we live in. For that security we pray; for that security we act—now and evermore.

XII-16-1942

The Four Freedoms

Ours is the responsibility of defending those principles which have come to us as our natural heritage, ours is the responsibility of passing them on—not only intact, but stronger than ever, to all the generations yet to come.

V-30-1941

＊　　＊　　＊

Just as our national policy in internal affairs has been based upon a decent respect for the rights and the dignity of all of our fellow men within our gates, so our national policy in foreign affairs has been based on a decent respect for the rights and the dignity of all nations, large and small.

＊　　＊　　＊

By an impressive expression of the public will and without regard to partisanship, we are committed to full support of all those resolute people everywhere who are resisting aggression. By this support we express our determination that the democratic cause shall prevail, and we strengthen the defense and the security of our own nation.

By an impressive expression of the public will and without regard to partisanship, we are committed to the proposition that principles of morality and considerations for our own security will never permit us to acquiesce in a peace dictated by aggressors and sponsored by appeasers. We know that enduring peace cannot be bought at the cost of other people's freedom.

The nation takes great satisfaction and much strength from the things which have been done to make its people conscious of their individual stake in the preservation of democratic life in America. Those things have toughened the fibre of our people, have renewed their faith and strengthened their devotion to the institutions we make ready to protect.

The basic things expected by our people of their political and economic systems are simple. They are:

Equality of opportunity for youth and for others.

Jobs for those who can work.

Security for those who need it.

The ending of special privileges for the few.

The preservation of civil liberties for all.

The enjoyment of the fruits of scientific progress in a wider and constantly rising standard of living.

In the future days which we seek to make secure, we look forward to a world founded upon four essential freedoms.

The first is freedom of speech and expression— everywhere in the world.

The second is freedom of every person to worship God in his own way—everywhere in the world.

The third is freedom from want, which, translated into world terms, means economic understandings which will secure to every nation a healthy peacetime life for its inhabitants—everywhere in the world.

The fourth is freedom from fear, which, translated into world terms, means a world-wide reduction of armaments to such a point and in such a thorough fashion that no nation will be in a position to commit an act of physical aggression against any neighbor—anywhere in the world.

That is no vision of a distant millennium. It is a definite basis for a kind of world attainable in our own time and generation. That kind of world is the very antithesis of the so-called "new order" of tyranny which the dictators seek to create with the crash of a bomb.

To that new order we oppose the greater conception—the moral order. A good society is able to face schemes of world domination and foreign revolutions alike without fear.

Since the beginning of our American history we have been engaged in change, in a perfect, peaceful revolution which goes on steadily, quietly, adjusting itself to changing conditions without the concentration camp or the quicklime in the ditch. The world order which we seek is the cooperation of free countries, working together in a friendly civilized society.

I-7-1941

*   *   *

The four freedoms of common humanity are as much elements of man's needs as air and sunshine, bread and salt. Deprive him of all these freedoms and he dies—deprive him of a part of them and a part of him withers. Give them to him in full and abundant measure and he will cross the threshold of a new age, the greatest age of man.

These freedoms are the rights of men of every creed and every race, wherever they live. This is their heritage long withheld. We of the United Nations have the power and the men and the will at last to assure man's heritage.

The belief in the four freedoms of common humanity—the belief in man, created free, in the image of God—is the crucial difference between ourselves and the enemies we face today. In it lies the absolute unity of our alliance, opposed to the oneness of the evil we hate. Here is our strength, the source and promise of victory.

VI-14-1942

❋   ❋   ❋

It is our determination to restore the conquered peoples to the dignity of human beings, masters of their own fate, entitled to freedom of speech, freedom of religion, freedom from want and freedom from fear.

VII-20-1943

❋   ❋   ❋

We must maintain the offensive against evil in all its forms. We must fight, to ensure that our children shall have and shall enjoy in peace their inalienable right to freedom of speech, freedom of religion, freedom from want, and freedom from fear.

IX-4-1942

The Enemy Within

America has always had—and America still has—
a small minority who assume that there are not
enough good things to go around to give that minority all that it wants and at the same time to give the
rest of America—the overwhelming majority of America—a humane and modern standard of living. Even
today that minority is shortsightedly sure that its interests must lie in exploiting all who labor on the farm
as well as in the mill and the mine.

But at the same time all over the country the unity
of interest of all common men and women—warm-
hearted, simple men and women, willing to live and
let live, whether in factory or on farm—grows steadily
more evident. Clearer every day is the one great lesson of history—the lesson taught by the Master of
Galilee—that the only road to peace and the only
road to a happier and better civilization is the road to
unity—the road called the "Highway of Fellowship."

IX-5-1938

*   *   *

When you come down to it, there is little difference between the feudal system and the Fascist system. If you believe in the one, you lean to the other.

With the overwhelming majority of the people of this land, I oppose feudalism. So do many among those who by virtue of their circumstances in life belong to the most prosperous 5 per cent of the population. Men and women in the professions, the overwhelming majority of the small storekeepers, a growing number of the bankers and business men—they are coming more and more to see that the continuation of the American system calls for the elimination of special privilege, the dissemination of the whole of the truth, and participation in prosperity by the people at the bottom of the ladder, as well as those in the middle and at the top.

One thing is certain—we are not going back to the old days. We are going forward to better days. We are calling for cooperation all along the line, and the cooperation is increasing because more and more people are coming to understand that abuses of the past which have been successfully eradicated are not going to be restored.

III-23-1938

* * *

The longer I live, the more am I convinced that there are two types of political leadership which are dangerous to the continuation of broad economic and social progress all along that long battlefront. The first type of political leadership which is dangerous to progress is represented by the man who harps on one or two remedies or proposals and claims that these one or two remedies will cure all our ills. The other type of dangerous leadership is represented by the man who says that he is in favor of progress but whose record shows that he hinders or hampers or tries to kill new measures of progress. He is that type of political leader who tells his friends that he does not like this or that or the other detail; and, at the same time, he utterly fails to offer a substitute that is practical or worthwhile.

VIII-11-1938

*　　*　　*

New ideas cannot be administered successfully by men with old ideas, for the first essential of doing a job well is the wish to see the job done at all.

Judge parties and candidates, not merely by what they promise, but by what they have done, by their records in office, by the kind of people they travel with, by the kind of people who finance and promote their campaigns. By their promoters ye shall know them.

XI-4-1938

*　　*　　*

There is, moreover, another enemy at home. That enemy is the mean and petty spirit that mocks at ideals, sneers at sacrifice and pretends that the American people can live by bread alone. If the spirit of God is not in us, and if we will not prepare to give all that we have and all that we are to preserve Christian civilization in our land, we shall go to destruction.

It is good and right that we should conserve these mountain heights of the old frontier for the benefit of the American people. But in this hour we have to safeguard a greater thing: the right of the people of this country to live as free men. Our vital task of conservation is to preserve the freedom that our forefathers won in this land, and the liberties that were proclaimed in our Declaration of Independence and embodied in our Constitution.

In these centuries of American civilization, greatly blessed by the bounties of nature, we succeeded in attaining liberty in Government and liberty of the person. In the process, in the light of past history, we realize now that we committed excesses which we are today seeking to atone for.

We used up or destroyed much of our natural heritage just because that heritage was so bountiful. We slashed our forests, we used our soil, we encouraged floods, we overconcentrated our wealth, we disregarded our unemployed—all of this so greatly that we were brought rather suddenly to face the fact that unless we gave thought to the lives of our children and grandchildren, they would no longer be able to live and to improve upon our American way of life.

In these later years we have tried sincerely and honestly to look ahead to the future years. We are at last definitely engaged in the task of conserving the bounties of nature, thinking in the terms of the whole of nature. We are trying at least to attain employment for all who would work and can work, and to provide a greater assurance of security throughout the life of the family.

From hard experience we know that the process is a long one, but most of us realize that if we can continue our effort without serious setbacks, the ideals of the American way of life can and will be attained by working everlastingly for the good of the whole and not for the good of any one privileged group.

So, from within our own borders, liberty through democracy can, I believe, be preserved in future years if we want to preserve it.

IX-2-1940

*   *   *

No people, least of all a democratic people, will be content to go without work or to accept some standard of living which obviously and woefully falls short of their capacity to produce. No people, least of all a people with our traditions of personal liberty, will endure the slow erosion of opportunity for the common man, the oppressive sense of helplessness under the domination of a few, which are overshadowing our whole economic life.

IV-29-1938

*   *   *

I am everlastingly angry only at those who assert vociferously that the Four Freedoms and the Atlantic Charter are nonsense because they are unattainable. If those people had lived a century and a half ago, they would have sneered and said that the Declaration of Independence was utter piffle. If they had lived nearly a thousand years ago, they would have laughed uproariously at the idea of the Magna Charta.

And if they had lived several thousand years ago, they would have derided Moses when he came from the mountains with the Ten Commandments.

IX-6-1943

*   *   *

We believe that people are even more important than machines. We believe that the material resources of America should serve the human resources of America.

We will not again allow people to be regimented by selfish minorities into bankruptcies and breadlines.

X-21-1936

*   *   *

The power of a few to manage the economic life of the nation must be diffused among the many or be transferred to the public and its democratically responsible government.

IV-29-1938

*   *   *

We understand the philosophy of those who offer resistance, of those who conduct a counter offensive against the American people's march of social progress. It is not an opposition which comes necessarily from wickedness—it is an opposition that comes from subconscious resistance to any measure that disturbs the position of privilege.

It is an unfortunate human failing that a full pocketbook often groans more loudly than an empty stomach.

I am, as you know, a firm believer in private enterprise and in private property. I am a firm believer in the American opportunity of men and women to rise in private enterprise.

But, of course, if private opportunity is to remain safe, average men and women must be able to have it as a part of their own individual satisfaction in life and their own stake in democracy.

XI-1-1940

* * *

Today we stand committed to the proposition that freedom is no half-and-half affair. If the average citizen is guaranteed equal opportunity in the polling place, he must have equal opportunity in the market place.

The economic royalists complain that we seek to overthrow the institutions of America. What they really complain of is that we seek to take away their power. Our allegiance to American institutions requires the overthrow of this kind of power. In vain they seek to hide behind the Flag and the Constitution. In their blindness they forget what the Flag and the Constitution stand for. Now, as always, they stand for democracy, not tyranny; for freedom, not subjection; and against a dictatorship by mob rule and the overprivileged alike.

But the resolute enemy within our gates is ever ready to beat down our words unless in greater courage we will fight for them.

The defeats and victories of these years have given

to us as a people a new understanding of our Government and of ourselves. Never since the early days of the New England town meeting have the affairs of Government been so widely discussed and so clearly appreciated. It has been brought home to us that the only effective guide for the safety of this most worldly of worlds, the greatest guide of all, is moral principle.

We do not see faith, hope and charity as unattainable ideals, but we use them as stout supports of a Nation fighting the fight for freedom in a modern civilization.

Faith—in the soundness of democracy in the midst of dictatorships.

Hope—renewed because we know so well the progress we have made.

Charity—in the true spirit of that grand old word. For charity literally translated from the original means love, the love that understands, that does not merely share the wealth of the giver, but in true sympathy and wisdom helps men to help themselves.

We seek not merely to make Government a mechanical implement, but to give it the vibrant personal character that is the very embodiment of human charity.

We are poor indeed if this Nation cannot afford to lift from every recess of American life the dread fear of the unemployed that they are not needed in the world. We cannot afford to accumulate a deficit in the books of human fortitude.

In the place of the palace of privilege we seek to build a temple out of faith and hope and charity.

It is a sobering thing, my friends, to be a servant of this great cause. We try in our daily work to remember that the cause belongs not to us, but to the people.

The standard is not in the hands of you and me alone. It is carried by America. We seek daily to profit from experience, to learn to do better as our task proceeds.

Governments can err, Presidents do make mistakes, but the immortal Dante tells us that divine justice weighs the sins of the cold-blooded and the sins of the warm-hearted in different scales.

Better the occasional faults of a Government that lives in a spirit of charity than the consistent omissions of a Government frozen in the ice of its own indifference.

There is a mysterious cycle in human events. To some generations much is given. Of other generations much is expected. This generation of Americans has a rendezvous with destiny.

In this world of ours in other lands, there are some people, who, in times past, have lived and fought for freedom, and seem to have grown too weary to carry on the fight. They have sold their heritage of freedom for the illusion of a living. They have yielded their democracy.

I believe in my heart that only our success can stir their ancient hope. They begin to know that here in America we are waging a great and successful war. It is not alone a war against want and destitution and economic demoralization. It is more than that; it is a war for the survival of democracy. We are fighting to save a great and precious form of government for ourselves and for the world.

VI-27-1936

*   *   *

In other countries the relationship of employer and employee has been more or less accepted as a class relationship not readily to be broken through. In this country we insist, as an essential of the American way of life, that the employer-employee relationship should be one between free men and equals. We refuse to regard those who work with hand or brain as different from or inferior to those who live from their property. We insist that labor is entitled to as much respect as property. But our workers with hand and brain deserve more than respect for their labor. They deserve practical protection to use their labor at a return adequate to support them at a decent and constantly rising standard of living, and to accumulate a margin of security against the inevitable vicissitudes of life.

The average man must have that twofold opportunity if we are to avoid the growth of a class-conscious society in this country.

There are those who fail to read both the signs of the times and American history. They would try to refuse the worker any effective power to bargain collectively, to earn a decent livelihood and to acquire security. It is those shortsighted ones, not labor, who threaten this country with that class dissension which in other countries has led to dictatorship and the establishment of fear and hatred as the dominant emotions in human life.

All American workers, brain workers and manual workers alike, and all the rest of us whose well-being depends on theirs, know that our needs are one in building an orderly economic democracy in which all can profit and in which all can be secure from the faulty economic direction.

IX-6-1936

*   *   *

I am only fighting for a free America—for a country in which *all* men and women have equal rights to liberty and justice.

I am fighting against the revival of Government by special privilege—Government by lobbyists—Government vested in the hands of those who favor and who would have us imitate the foreign dictatorships.

I am fighting, as I always have fought, for the rights of the little man as well as the big man—for the weak as well as the strong, for those who are helpless as well as for those who can help themselves.

I am fighting to keep this nation prosperous and at peace, and to keep foreign conceptions of Government out of our own United States.

I am fighting for these great and good causes. I am fighting to defend them against the power and might of those who now rise up to challenge them.

And I will not stop fighting.

XI-1-1940

*   *   *

In our generation, a new idea has come to dominate thought about government, the idea that the resources of the nation can be made to produce a far higher standard of living for the masses of the people if only government is intelligent and energetic in giving the right direction to economic life.

That idea—or more properly that ideal—is wholly justified by the facts. It cannot be thrust aside by those who want to go back to the conditions of years ago or even preserve the conditions of today. It puts all forms of government to their proof.

That ideal makes understandable the demands of labor for shorter hours and higher wages, the demands of farmers for a more stable income, the demands of the great majority of business men for relief from disruptive trade practices, the demands of all for the end of that kind of license, often mistermed "Liberty," which permits a handful of the population to take far more than its tolerable share from the rest of the people.

IX-17-1937

*   *   *

The men who wrote the constitution were the men who fought the Revolution. They had watched a weak emergency government almost lose the war, and continue economic distress among thirteen little republics, at peace but without effective national government.

So when these men planned a new government, they drew the kind of agreement which men make when they really want to work together under it for a very long time.

For the youngest of nations they drew what is to-day the oldest written instrument under which men have continuously lived together as a nation.

The Constitution of the United States was a lay-man's document, not a lawyer's contract. *That* cannot be stressed too often. Madison, most responsible for it, was not a lawyer; nor was Washington or Franklin, whose sense of the give-and-take of life had kept the Convention together.

IX-17-1937

*　*　*

The present government of the United States has never taken away and never will take away any liberty from any minority, unless it be a minority which so abuses its liberty as to do positive and definite harm to its neighbors constituting the majority. But the government of the United States refused to forget that the Bill of Rights was put into the Constitution not only to protect minorities against intolerance of majorities, but to protect majorities against the enthrone-ment of minorities.

IV-17-1937

*　*　*

In considering the present and the future of American politics or policies, you have the right and the duty to say to those who want to stand still—"Have you no program other than standing still? We are not satisfied if you tell us glibly that you believe in taking care of old people, that you want the young people to have jobs, that you want everybody to have a job, that you

believe in a fairer distribution of wealth—we insist
in addition that you give us specifications of how you
would do it if you were in power."

Do not let the reactionaries and the conservatives
get away with fine phrases. Pin them down and make
them tell you just how they would do it.

VIII-8-1939

* * *

Military victory is not enough. We shall not have com-
pleted the defense of our way of life until we
also solve the second task, the reconstruction of an
economy in which every one willing to work can find
for himself a place in productive employment. The
enemy, though beaten on the battlefields, may still
arise in our midst if we fail in the task of reconstruction.

I-10-44

Government with a Soul

It is always a good thing to look beneath the surface of things, to look into men's hearts. Do they really mean what they say—or are they the kind that profess great devotion to the cause of bettering the lot of their fellow countrymen, and, when the time for action comes, find all kinds of reasons why they cannot support the action proposed?

In the same way we find others who seek office, sincerely or otherwise, on perfectly impossible pledges and platforms—people with panaceas for reforming the world overnight—people who are not practical in an age that must be and can be both practical and progressive. Theodore Roosevelt was perhaps a bit rough in his language when he referred to such people as "the lunatic fringe." Of course, strictly speaking, they are not lunatics, but in many cases a little push would shove them over the line.

During these past years the people of this Nation have definitely said "yes"—with no "but" about it—to the old Biblical question, "Am I my brother's keeper?" In these years I sense a growing devotion to the teachings of the Scriptures, to the quickening of religion, to a greater religion, to a greater willingness on the part of the individual to help his neighbor and to live less unto and for himself alone.

America needs a government of constant progress along liberal lines. America requires that this progress be sane and that this progress be honest. America calls for government with a soul.

VII-9-1938

* * *

The problems which we all face—the problems of so-called economics, the problems that are called monetary problems, the problems of unemployment, the problems of industry and agriculture—we shall not succeed in solving unless the people of this country hold the spiritual values of the country just as high as they do the economic values.

IX-29-1933

* * *

Without spiritual armor we cannot hope to win the war. Without spiritual armor we cannot be worthy of the victory our men are purchasing at a great cost on the battle-field. Without spiritual armor we cannot hope to play an honorable and responsible part in the establishment of world peace.

VI-31-1943

* * *

All of recorded history bears witness that the human race has made true advancement only as it has appreciated spiritual values.

V-4-1941

* * *

Our strength is measured not only in terms of the might of our armaments. It is measured not only in terms of the horse-power of our machines.

The true measure of our strength lies deeply imbedded in the social and economic justice of the system in which we live.

For you can build ships and tanks and planes and guns galore; but they will not be enough. You must place behind them an invincible faith in the institutions which they have been built to defend.

X-2-1940

* * *

For more than three centuries we Americans have been building on this continent a free society, a society in which the promise of the human spirit may find fulfillment. Commingled here are the blood and genius of all the peoples of the world who have sought this promise.

We have built well. We are continuing our efforts to bring the blessings of a free society, of a free and productive economic system, to every family in the land. This is the promise of America.

It is this that we must continue to build—this that we must continue to defend.

It is the task of our generation, yours and mine. But we build and defend not for our generation alone. We defend the foundations laid down by our fathers. We build a life for generations yet unborn. We defend and we build a way of life, not for America alone, but for all mankind.

V-26-1940

*   *   *

Human kindness has never weakened the stamina or softened the fiber of a free people. A nation does not have to be cruel in order to be tough. The vigorous expression of our American community spirit is truly important.

The ancient injunction to love thy neighbor as thyself is still the force that animates our faith—a faith that we are determined shall live and conquer in a world poisoned by hatred and ravaged by war.

X-13-1940

*   *   *

In matters of social welfare we should keep in sight of the fact that we are not dealing with "units," "individuals" or with "economic men." We are dealing with persons. Human personality is something sacred. It enjoys the light of reason and liberty. It grows by rising above material things and wedding itself to spiritual ideals. Our social order is worthy of human beings only in so far as it recognizes the inherent value of human personality. Our cities, our States and our Nations exist not for themselves but for men and women. We cannot be satisfied with any form of society in which human personality is submerged.

V-23-1936

❃   ❃   ❃

Let us not be afraid to help each other—let us never forget that government is *ourselves* and not an alien power over us. The ultimate rulers of our democracy are not a President and Senators and Congressmen and Government officials but the voters of this country.

VII-8-1938

❃   ❃   ❃

We don't want and we are not going to copy other forms of government—ours is good enough for us.

VII-12-1938

❃   ❃   ❃

A Government can be no better than the public opinion which sustains it.

I-8-1936

For Peace I Shall Labor

Today we seek a moral basis for peace. It cannot be a real peace if it fails to recognize brotherhood. It cannot be a lasting peace if the fruit of it is oppression, or starvation, or cruelty, or human life dominated by armed camps. It cannot be a sound peace if small nations must live in fear of powerful neighbors. It cannot be a moral peace if freedom from invasion is sold for tribute. It cannot be an intelligent peace if it denies free passage to that knowledge of those ideals which permit men to find common ground. It cannot be a righteous peace if worship of God is denied.

III-16-1940

    ❄   ❄   ❄

I have seen war. I have seen war on land and sea. I have seen blood running from the wounded. I have seen men coughing out their gassed lungs. I have seen the dead in the mud. I have seen cities destroyed. I have seen two hundred limping, exhausted men come out of line—the survivors of a regiment of one thousand that went forward forty hours before. I have seen children starving. I have seen the agony of mothers and wives. I hate war.

VIII-14-1936

* * *

There is a solidarity and interdependence about the modern world, both technically and morally, which makes it impossible for any nation completely to isolate itself from economic and political upheavals in the rest of the world, especially when such upheavals appear to be spreading and not declining. There can be no stability or peace either within nations except under laws and moral standards adhered to by all. International anarchy destroys every foundation for peace. It jeopardizes either the immediate or the future security of every nation, large or small. It is, therefore, a matter of vital interest and concern to the people of the United States that the sanctity of international treaties and the maintenance of international morality be restored.

X-5-1937

* * *

The blame for the danger to world peace lies not in the world population but in the political leaders of that population.

XII-28-1933

* * *

It is for peace that I have labored and for peace that I shall labor all the days of my life.

X-23-1940

*   *   *

We in this Nation of many States have found the way by which men of many racial origins may live together in peace.

If the human race as a whole is to survive, the world must find the way by which men and nations can live together in peace. We cannot accept the doctrine that war must be forever a part of man's destiny.

XI-2-1940

*   *   *

We do not expect a new Heaven and a new Earth overnight, but in our own land, and other lands— wherever men of good will listen to our appeal—we shall work as best we can with the instruments at hand to banish hatred, greed and covetousness from the heart of mankind.

XII-24-1938

*   *   *

We believe in democracy; we believe in freedom; we believe in peace. We offer to every Nation of the world the handclasp of the good neighbor. Let those who wish our friendship look us in the eye and take our hand.

VIII-14-1936

*   *   *

We seek no gain at the expense of others. We threaten no one, nor do we tolerate threats from others. No nation is more deeply dedicated to the ways of peace. No nation is fundamentally stronger to resist aggression.

The American people are not easily fooled; they are hard-headed realists and they fear no one.

X-26-1941

* * *

I want our great democracy to be wise enough to realize that aloofness from war is not promoted by unawareness of war. In a world of mutual suspicions, peace must be affirmatively reached for. It cannot just be wished for. It cannot just be waited for.

X-12-1937

* * *

We as a Nation seek spiritual union with all who love freedom. Of many bloods and of diverse national origins, we stand before the world today as one people united in a common determination. That determination is to uphold the ideal of human society which makes conscience superior to brute strength, the ideal which would substitute freedom for force in the governments of the world.

X-11-1937

* * *

It is becoming increasingly clear that peace by fear has no higher or more enduring quality than peace by the sword.

There can be no peace if the reign of law is to be replaced by a recurrent sanctification of sheer force.

There can be no peace if national policy adopts as a deliberate instrument the threat of war.

There can be no peace if national policy adopts as a deliberate instrument the dispersion all over the world of millions of helpless and persecuted wanderers with no place to lay their heads.

There can be no peace if humble men and women are not free to think their own thoughts, to express their own feelings, to worship God.

X-26-1938

* * *

I wish I could keep war from all Nations; but that is beyond my power. I can at least make certain that no act of the United States helps to produce or to promote war. I can at least make clear that the conscience of America revolts against war and that any Nation which provokes war forfeits the sympathy of the people of the United States.

VIII-14-1936

* * *

In the field of world policy I would dedicate this nation to the policy of the good neighbor—the neighbor who resolutely respects himself and, because he does so, respects the rights of others—the neighbor who respects his obligations and respects the sanctity of his agreements in and with a world of neighbors.

VIII-14-1936

* * *

The development of civilization and of human welfare is based on the acceptance by individuals of certain fundamental decencies in their relations with each other.

X-12-1937

*   *   *

There is a trend in the world away from the observance both of the letter and the spirit of treaties. We propose to observe, as we have in the past, our own treaty obligations to the limit; but we cannot be certain of reciprocity on the part of others.

Disregard for treaty obligations seems to have followed the surface trend away from the democratic representative form of government. It would seem, therefore, that world peace through international agreements is most safe in the hands of democratic representative governments—or, in other words, peace is most greatly jeopardized in and by those nations where democracy has been discarded or has never developed.

I have used the words "surface trend," for I still believe that civilized man increasingly insists and in the long run will insist on genuine participation in his own government. Our people believe that over the years democracies of the world will survive, and that democracy will be restored or established in those nations which today know it not. In that faith lies the future peace of mankind.

I-3-1938

True Education

The qualities of a true education remain what they were when Washington insisted upon its importance.

First among these qualities is a sense of fair play among men.

As education grows, men come to recognize their essential dependence one upon the other. There is revealed to them the true nature of society and a Government which, in a large measure, culminates in the art of human cooperation.

The second great attribute of education is peculiarly appropriate to a great democracy. It is a sense of equality among men when they are dealing with the things of the mind. Inequality may linger in the world of material things, but great music, great literature, great art and the wonders of science are, and should be, open to all.

Finally, a true education depends upon freedom in the pursuit of truth. No group and no Government can properly prescribe precisely what should constitute the body of knowledge with which true education is concerned. The truth is found when men are free to pursue it. Genuine education is present only when the springs from which knowledge comes are pure. It is this belief in the freedom of the mind, written into our fundamental law, and observed in our everyday dealings with the problems of life, that distinguishes us as a nation, the United States of America, above every Nation in the world.

In our ability to keep pure the sources of knowledge, in our mind's freedom to winnow the chaff from the good grain, in the even temper and in the calmness of our everyday relationships, in our willingness to face the details of fact and the needs of temporary emergencies—in all of these lie our future and our children's future.

"On your own heads, in your own hands, the sin and the saving lies!"

II-22-1936

*   *   *

The great achievements of science and even of art can be used in one way or another to destroy as well as to create; they are only instruments by which men try to do things they most want to do. If death is desired, science can do that. If a full, rich, and useful life is sought, science can do that also.

V-10-1940

*   *   *

As we grow older we realize our inability to meet perfection, the happier we can and should be in everything that we do to make life a little better—to use the vehicles of science and cooperation to improve the lot of those who need it most.

I-30-1940

*   *   *

American education must prepare men for freedom, equip them to create and maintain freedom, so ground them in a sense of value that they see in free men the ultimate good. In so far as we extend the democratic ideal and make it the practice of common life, we create an America about which the truth need but be told. In so far as education gives the mind and will essential to the task, it is but necessary to publicize its intrinsic nature.

VIII-12-1941

*   *   *

Art in America has always belonged to the people and has never been the property of an academy or a class.

In the future we must seek more widespread popular understanding and appreciation of the arts. Many of our great cities provide the facilities for such appreciation. But we all know that because of their lack of size and riches the smaller communities are in most cases denied this opportunity. That is why I give special emphasis to the need of giving these smaller communities the visual chance to get to know modern art.

As in our democracy we enjoy the right to believe in different religious creeds or in none, so can American artists express themselves with complete freedom from the strictures of dead artistic tradition or political ideology. While American artists have discovered a new obligation to the society in which they live, they have no compulsion to be limited in method or manner of expression.

V-10-1939

* * *

The only real capital of a nation is its natural resources and its human beings. So long as we take care of and make the most of both of them, we shall survive as a strong nation, a successful nation and a progressive nation—whether or not the bookkeepers say other kinds of budgets are from time to time out of balance.

* * *

Freedom to learn is the first necessity of guaranteeing that man himself shall be self-reliant enough to be free.

Such things did not need as much emphasis a generation ago; but when the clock of civilization can be turned back by burning libraries, by exiling scientists, artists, musicians, writers and teachers, by dispersing universities, and by censoring news and literature and art, an added burden is placed upon those countries where the torch of free thought and free learning still burns bright.

If the fires of freedom and civil liberties burn low in other lands, they must be made brighter in our own.

There may be times when men and women in the turmoil of change lose touch with the civilized gains of centuries of education: but the gains of education are never really lost. Books may be burned and cities sacked, but truth, like the yearning for freedom, lives in the hearts of humble men and women. The ultimate victory of tomorrow is with democracy, and through democracy with education, for no people in all the world can be kept eternally ignorant or eternally enslaved.

VI-30-1938

*　　*　　*

Democracy cannot succeed unless those who express their choice are prepared to choose wisely. The real safeguard of democracy, therefore, is education. It has been well said that no system of government gives so much to the individual or exacts so much as a democracy. Upon our educational system must largely depend the perpetuity of those institutions upon which our freedom and our security rest. To prepare each citizen to choose wisely and to enable him to choose freely are paramount functions of the schools in a democracy.

IX-27-1938

*　　*　　*

In all our plans we are guided, and will continue to be guided, by the fundamental belief that the American farmer, living on his own land, remains our ideal of self-reliance and of spiritual balance—the source from which the reservoirs of the Nation's strength are constantly renewed. It is from the men and women of our farms, living close to the soil, that this Nation, like the Greek giant Antaeus, touches Mother Earth and rises with strength renewed a hundred fold.

We want to perpetuate that ideal, we want to perpetuate it under modern conditions, so that man may be strong in the ancient virtues and yet lay hold of the advantages which science and new knowledge offer to a well-rounded life.

X-10-1936

*   *   *

The inheritance which we had hoped to share with every nation of the world is, for the moment, left largely in our keeping: and it is our compelling duty to guard and enrich that legacy, to preserve it for a world which must be reborn from the ashes of the present disaster.

V-10-1940

*   *   *

. . . *We* all recognize that the spirit within the home is the most important influence in the growth of the child. In family life the child should first learn confidence in his own powers, respect for the feelings and the rights of others, the feeling of security and mutual good will and faith in God. Here he should find a common bond between the interests of the individual and the interests of the group. Mothers and fathers, by the kind of life they build within the four walls of the home, are largely responsible for the future social and public life of the country.

Just as we cannot take care of the child apart from

the family, so his welfare is bound up with a lot of other institutions that influence his development— the school, the church, the agencies that offer useful and happy activities and interests for leisure time. The work of all these institutions needs to be harmonized so as to give our children rounded growth with the least possible conflict and loss of effort. And the money and hard work that go into these public and private enterprises are, again, repaid many times.

Religion, religion especially, helps children to appreciate life in its wholeness, to develop a deep sense of the sacredness of human personality. In view of the estimate that perhaps one-half of the children of America are having no regular religious instruction, it seems to me important to consider how provision can best be made for some kind of religious training. We can do it because we are capable of keeping in mind both the wisdom of maintaining the separation of Church and State and, at the same time, the great importance of religion in personal and social living.

I-19-1940

* * *

We and most of the people in the World, still believe in a civilization of construction and not destruction. We, and most of the people in the world, still believe that men and women have an inherent right to hew out the patterns of their own individual lives, just so long as they as individuals do not harm their fellow beings. We call this ideal by many terms which are synonymous—we call it individual liberty, we call it civil liberty and, I think, best of all, we call it democracy.

Until now we permit ourselves by common consent to search for truth, to teach the truth as we see it—and by learning a little here and a little there, and by teaching a little there, to allow the normal processes of truth to keep growing for the well-being of our fellow men. In our search and in our teachings we are a part of a great adventure—an exciting adventure—which gives to us even a larger satisfaction than our forefathers had when they were in the midst of the adventure of settling the Americas from the Old World. We feel that we are building human progress by conquering disease, poverty and discomfort, and by improving science and culture, removing one by one the many cruelties, crudities and barbarities of less civilized eras.

In contrast to that rather simple picture of our ideals, in other parts of the world, teachers and scholars are not permitted to search for truth, lest the truth, when made known, might not suit the designs of their masters. Too often they are not allowed to teach the truth as they see it, because truth might make men free. They become objects of suspicion if they speak openly, if they show an interest in new truth, for their tongues and minds are supposed to be mobilized for other ends.

V-10-1940

*   *   *

Benjamin Franklin realized too that while basic principles of natural science, of morality and of the science of society were eternal and immutable, the application of these principles necessarily changes with the patterns of living conditions from generation to generation. I am certain that he would insist, were he with us today, that it is the whole duty of the philosopher and the educator to apply the eternal ideals of truth and goodness and justice in terms of the present and not in terms of the past. Growth and change are the law of all alike. Yesterday's answers are inadequate for today's problems—just as the solutions of today will not fill the needs of tomorrow.

Eternal truths will be neither true nor eternal unless they have fresh meaning for every new social situation.

It is the function of education, the function of all of the great institutions of learning in the United States, to provide continuity for our national life—to transmit to youth the best of our culture that has been tested in the fire of history. It is equally the obligation of education to train the minds and talents of our youth; to improve, through creative citizenship, our American institutions in accord with the requirements of the future.

IV-20-1940

*　　*　　*　　*

This is no time for any man to withdraw into some ivory tower and proclaim the right to hold himself aloof from the problems and the agonies of his societies. The times call for bold belief that the world can be changed by man's endeavor, and that this endeavor can lead to something new and better. No man can sever the bonds that unite him to his society simply by averting his eyes. He must ever be receptive and sensitive to the new; and have sufficient courage and skill to face novel facts and to deal with them.

If democracy is to survive, it is the task of men of thought, as well as men of action, to put aside pride and prejudice; and with courage and single-minded devotion—and above all with humility—to find the truth and teach the truth that shall keep men free.

We may find in that sense of purpose, the personal peace, not of repose, but of effort, the keen satisfaction of doing, the deep feeling of achievement for something far beyond ourselves, the knowledge that we build more gloriously than we know.

IV-20-1940

Dynamic Democracy

They do not believe in democracy—I do. My anchor is democracy—and more democracy. I am of the firm belief that the Nation, by an overwhelming majority, supports my opposition to the vesting of supreme power in the hands of any class, numerous but select.

* * *

Under democratic government the poorest are no longer necessarily the most ignorant part of society. I agree with the saying of one of our famous statesmen who devoted himself to the principle of majority rule: "I respect the aristocracy of learning; I deplore the plutocracy of wealth; but thank God for the democracy of the heart."

I seek no change in the form of American government. Majority rule must be preserved as the safeguard of both liberty and civilization.

Under it property can be secure; under it abuses can end; under it order can be maintained—and all of this for the simple, cogent reason that to the average of our citizenship can be brought a life of greater opportunity, of greater security, of greater happiness.

VIII-18-1937

* * *

No, democracy is not dying.

We know it because we have seen it revive and grow.

We know it can't die because it is built on the unhampered initiative of individual men and women joined together in a common enterprise—an enterprise undertaken and carried through by the free expression of a free majority.

We know it because democracy alone, of all forms of government, enlists the full force of men's enlightened will.

We know it because democracy alone has constructed an unlimited civilization capable of infinite progress in the improvement of human life.

We know it because if we look below the surface, we sense it still spreading on every continent; for it is the most humane, the most advantageous, and in the end the most unconquerable of all forms of human society.

A nation, like a person, has a body, a body that must be fed and clothed and housed, invigorated and rested, in a manner that measures up to the standards of our time.

A nation, like a person, has a mind—a mind that must be kept informed and alert, that must know itself, that understands the hope and the needs of its neighbors—all the other nations that live within the narrowing circle of the world.

A nation, like a person, has something deeper, something more permanent, something larger than the sum of all its parts. It is that something which matters most to its future, which calls forth the most sacred guarding of its present.

It is a thing for which we find it difficult—even impossible—to hit upon a single, simple word.

And yet we all understand what it is—the spirit— the faith of America. It is the product of centuries. It was born in the multitudes of those who came from many lands—some of high degree, but mostly plain people—who sought here, early and late, to find freedom more freely.

The democratic aspiration is no mere recent phase in human history. It is human history. It permeated the ancient life of early peoples. It blazed anew in the Middle Ages. It was written in Magna Charta.

In the Americas its impact has been irresistible. America has been the new world in all tongues, and to all peoples, not because this continent was a new found land, but because all who came here believed they could create upon this continent a new life—a life that should be new in freedom.

Its vitality was written into our Mayflower Compact, into the Declaration of Independence, into the Constitution of the United States, into the Gettysburg Address.

Those who first came here to carry out the longings of their spirit and the millions who followed and the stock that sprang from them—all have moved forward constantly and consistently toward an ideal which in itself has gained stature and clarity with each generation.

The destiny of America was proclaimed in words of prophecy spoken by our first President in his first inaugural in 1789—words almost directed, it would seem, to this year: "The preservation of the sacred fire of literature and the destiny of the republican model of government are justly considered . . . deeply, . . . finally, staked on the experiment intrusted to the hands of the American people."

We do not retreat. We are not content to stand still. As Americans, we go forward, in the service of our country, by the will of God.

I-20-1941

＊   ＊   ＊

That propaganda repeats and repeats that democracy is a decadent form of Government. They tell us that our old democratic ideal, our old traditions of civil liberties, are things of the past.

We reject that thought. We say that we are the future. We say that the direction in which they would lead us is backward, not forward—backward to the bondage of the Pharaohs, backward to the slavery of the Middle Ages.

The command of the democratic faith has been ever onward and upward. Never have free men been satisfied with the mere maintenance of any status quo, however comfortable or secure it may have seemed at the moment.

We have always held to the hope, the belief, the conviction, that there is a better life, a better world, beyond the horizon.

That fire of freedom was in the eyes of Washington, and Bolivar, and San Martin, and Artigas, and Juarez, and Bernardo O'Higgins, and all the brave, rugged, ragged men who followed them in the wars of independence.

That fire burns in the eyes of those who are fighting for freedom in lands across the sea.

X-12-1940

*　　*　　*

I speak bluntly. I speak the love the American people have for freedom and liberty and decency and humanity.

X-12-1940

*　　*　　*

Too many of those who prate about saving democracy are really only interested in saving things as they were. Democracy should concern itself also with things as they ought to be.

I am not talking mere idealism; I am expressing realistic necessity.

XI-4-1938

*　　*　　*

America . . . is a country which talks out its problems in the open, where any man can hear them.

The decisions of our democracy may be slowly arrived at, but when that decision is made, it is proclaimed not with the voice of any one man but with the voice of 130,000,000. It is binding on all of us.

V-16-1941

*   *   *

All of the great freedoms which form the basis of our American democracy are part and parcel of that concept of free election, with free expression of political choice between candidates of political parties. For such elections guarantee that there can be no possibility of stifling freedom of speech, freedom of the press and the air, freedom of worship.

V-30-1941

*   *   *

Sometimes men wonder overmuch what they will receive for what they are giving in the service of a democracy—whether it is worth the cost to share in that struggle which is a part of the business of representative government. But the reward of that effort is to feel that they have been a part of great things, that they have helped to build, that they have had their share in the great battles of their generation.

XI-2-1936

*   *   *

Freedom of speech is of no use to a man who has nothing to say.

Freedom of worship is of no use to a man who has lost his God.

Democracy, to be dynamic, must provide for its citizens opportunity as well as freedom.

X-2-1940

*   *   *

The right of freedom of worship would mean nothing without freedom of speech. And the rights of free labor as we know them today could not survive without the rights of free enterprise.

That is the indestructible bond that is between us, between all of us Americans—interdependence of interests, privileges, oppositions, respects, interdependence of rights.

IX-2-1941

*   *   *

Events in this world of ours today are making the vast majority of our citizens think more and more clearly about the manner of the growth of their liberty and freedom, and how hard their people in the olden days fought and worked to win and to hold the privilege of free Government.

With the gaining of our political freedom you will remember that there came a conflict between the point of view of Alexander Hamilton, sincerely believing in the superiority of Government by a small group of public-spirited and usually wealthy citizens, and, on the other hand, the point of view of Thomas Jefferson, an advocate of Government by representatives chosen by all the people, an advocate of the universal right of free thought, free personal living, free religion, free expression of opinion and, above all, the right of free universal suffrage.

Many of the Jeffersonian school of thought were frank to admit the high motives and disinterestedness of Hamilton and his school. Many Americans of those days were willing to concede that if Government could be guaranteed to be kept always on the high level of unselfish service suggested by the Hamiltonians there would be nothing to fear. For the very basis of the Hamiltonian philosophy was that through a system of elections every four years, limited to the votes of the most highly educated and the most successful citizens, the best of those qualified to govern could always be selected.

It was, however, with rare perspicuity, as time has shown, that Jefferson pointed out that, on the doctrine of sheer human frailty, the Hamilton theory was bound to develop, in the long run, into Government by selfishness or Government for personal gain or Government by class, that would ultimately lead to the abolishment of free elections. For he recognized that it was our system of free unhampered elections which was the surest guaranty of popular Government. Just so long as the voters of the Nation, regardless of higher education or property possessions, were free to exercise their choice in the polling place without hindrance, the country would have no cause to fear the head of tyranny.

. . . The older I grow, the less omniscient I become in regard to economics, and I think most of us do. As in the days of Hamilton, we of our own generation should give those who demand government by the few all credit for pure intention and high ideals. Nevertheless, their type of political thinking could easily lead to Government by selfish seekers for power and riches and glory. For the great danger is that once the Government falls into the hands of a few elite, curtailment or even abolition of free elections might be adopted as the means of keeping them in power.

As long as periodic free elections survive, no set of people can permanently control Government. In the maintenance of free elections rests the complete and the enduring safety of our form of Government.

No dictator in history has ever dared to run the gauntlet of a really free election.

IX-20-1940

We Belong to Many Races

The tragedies of this distractful world have weighed heavily on all of us.

But—there is revival for every one of us in the sight of our own national community.

In our own American community we have sought to submerge all the old hatreds, all the old fears, of the old world.

We are Anglo-Saxon and Latin, we are Irish and Teuton and Jewish and Scandinavian and Slav—we are American. We belong to many races and colors and creeds—we are American.

And it seems to me that we are most completely, most loudly, most proudly American around Election Day.

Because it is then that we can assert ourselves— voters and candidates alike. We can assert the most glorious, the most encouraging fact in all the world to-day—the fact that democracy is alive—and going strong.

We are telling the world that we are free—and we intend to remain free and at peace.

We are free to live and love and laugh.

We face the future with confidence and courage. We are American.

X-30-1940

*   *   *

As to the humorless theory—that we are "hybrid and undynamic—mongrel and corrupt," and that, therefore, we can have no common tradition—let them look at most gatherings of Americans and study the common purpose that animates those gatherings. Let them look at any church sociable in any small town— at any fraternal convention, or meeting of doctors or mine workers—at any cheering section of any football game; let them look with especial attention at the crowds which will gather in and around every polling place on November fifth. Let them observe the unconquerable vitality of democracy. It is the very mingling of races dedicated to common ideals which creates and recreates our vitality.

In every representative American meeting there will be men and women and children with names like Jackson and Lincoln and Isaac and Schultz and O'Brien and Stuyvesant and Olson and Kovacs and Satori and Jones and Smith. These varied Americans with varied backgrounds are all immigrants or the descendants of immigrants. All of them are inheritors of the same stalwart tradition—a tradition of unusual enterprise, of adventurousness, of courage "to pull up stakes and git moving." That has been the great, compelling force in our history. Our continent, our hemisphere, has been populated by people who wanted life better than the life they had previously known. They were willing to undergo all conceivable perils, all conceivable hardships, to achieve the better life. They were animated just as we are animated by this compelling force today. It is what makes us Americans.

The bold and the adventurous men, of many racial origins, were united in their determination to build a system which guaranteed freedom—for themselves and for all future generations. They built a system in which Government and people are one—a nation which is a partnershhip—and can continue as a partnership.

That is our strength today.

X-24-1940

* * *

We have steadily sought to keep mobilized the greatest force of all—religious faith, devotion to God.

Our Government is working at all times with representatives of the Catholic, Protestant, and Jewish faiths. Without these three, all three of them, without them working with us toward that great end, things would not be as clear or as easy.

Shadows, however, are still heavy over the faith and the hope of mankind.

We—who walk in the ways of peace and freedom and light—have seen the tragedies enacted in one free land after another.

We have not been blind to the causes or the conse-
quences of these tragedies.

We guard ourselves against all evils—spiritual as
well as material—which may beset us. We guard
against the forces of anti-Christian aggression, which
may attack us from without, and the forces of igno-
rance and fear which may corrupt us from within.

We go forward with firm faith. And we shall continue to go forward in peace.

X-28-1940

* * *

Out of the dregs of present disaster we can distill some
real achievements in human progress.

This problem involves no one race group—no one
religious faith. It is the problem of all groups and all
faiths. It is not enough to indulge in horrified humani-
tarianism, empty resolutions, golden rhetoric and
pious words. We must face it actively if the democratic principle based on respect and human dignity is
to survive, and if world order, which rests on security
of the individual, is to be restored.

Remembering the words written on the Statue of
Liberty, let us lift a lamp beside new golden doors and
build new refuges for the tired, for the poor, for the
huddled masses yearning to be free.

X-17-1939

* * *

The service of democracy must be something much
more than mere lip-service.

It is a living thing—a human thing—compounded of brains and muscles and heart and soul. The service of democracy is the birthright of every citizen, the white and the colored; the Protestant, the Catholic, the Jew; the sons and daughters of every country in the world, who make up the people of this land. Democracy is every man and woman who loves freedom and serves freedom.

XI-4-1940

*　　*　　*

The lesson of religious toleration—a toleration which recognizes complete liberty of human thought, liberty of human conscience—is one which, by precept and example, must be inculcated in the hearts and minds of all Americans if the institutions of our democracy are to be maintained and perpetuated.

III-30-1937

*　　*　　*

This nation was created to insure the things that unite and to eliminate the things that divide.

V-17-1940

*　　*　　*

Every American takes pride in our tradition of hospitality to men of all races and of all creeds. One of the great achievements of the American commonwealth has been the fact that race groups which were divided abroad are united here. Enmities and antagonisms were forgotten; former opponents met here as friends. Groups which had fought each other overseas here work together; their children intermarry; they have all made contributions to democracy and peace.

Because of the very greatness of this achievement, we must be constantly vigilant against the attacks of intolerance and injustice. We must scrupulously guard the civil rights and civil liberties of all citizens, whatever their background. We must remember that any oppression, any injustice, any hatred, is a wedge designed to attack our civilization. If reason is to prevail against intolerance, we must always be on guard.

I-9-1940

*   *   *

We are a nation of many nationalities, many races, many religions—bound together by a single unity, the unity of freedom and equality.

Whoever seeks to set one nationality against another, seeks to degrade all nationalities.

Whoever seeks to set one race against another seeks to enslave all races.

Whoever seeks to set one religion against another, seeks to destroy all religion.

XI-1-1940

*   *   *

In every battalion, in every ship's crew you will find every kind of American citizen representing every occupation, every section, every origin, every religion and every political viewpoint.

Ask them what they are fighting for and every one of them will say: "I am fighting for my country." Ask them what they really mean by that, and you will get what, on the surface, may seem to be a wide variety of answers.

One will say that he is fighting for the right to say what he pleases and to read and listen to what he likes.

Another will say he is fighting because he never wants to see the swastika flying over the old First Baptist Church on Elm Street.

Another soldier will say that he is fighting for the right to work to earn three square meals a day for himself and his folks.

Another one will say he is fighting in this world war so that his children and his grandchildren will not have to go back to Europe, or Africa, or Asia, or the Solomon Islands, to do this ugly job all over again, and all these answers really add up to the same thing: every American fights for freedom. And today the personal freedom of every American and his family depends, and in the future will increasingly depend, upon the freedom of his neighbors in other lands.

For today the whole world is one neighborhood. That is why this war, that had its beginnings in seemingly remote areas, China, Poland, has spread to every continent and most of the islands of the sea, involving the lives and the liberties of the entire human race.

II-13-1943